REPORT OF
THE THIRTY-NINTH ROUND TABLE
ON TRANSPORT ECONOMICS

held in Paris on 19th and 20th October, 1977
on the following topic:

ECONOMIC
PROSPECTS
FOR
RAILWAYS

EUROPEAN CONFERENCE OF MINISTERS OF TRANSPORT

LIBRARY
AUG 1 7 1981
UNIVERSITY OF THE PACIFIC

***

TABLE OF CONTENTS

The problems of the railways are too familiar and topical for
their importance and urgency to need any proof, but this Round Table
has a particular interest for the ECMT because it provided one of the
basic documents referred to by the Council of Ministers for their discussion of the subject at the Session held on 6th December 1977.

These documents were as follows:

1. The Report of the Railways Committee setting out the views
   of the responsible national government experts.
2. A summary of the conclusions of that report and a summary
   of the issues arising from it.
3. The conclusions of the Round Table as set out at the end
   of this paper.

The papers put before the Ministers thus included the opinions of
officials with direct responsibility and those of persons who were not
under that constraint.

While the conclusions on both sides were alike on many points
there were nevertheless differences of emphasis or attitude with
policy-makers being more interested in immediate problems and researchers
more concerned with the longer term, and this is why the present Round
Table will probably be used again as a guide for future discussions.

In view of the complementarity of the two approaches the ECMT will
tend in future to deal with important problems from the twofold angle
of policy-making and research.

<u>ECONOMIC PROSPECTS FOR RAILWAYS</u>

Professor Dr. G. ABERLE
University of Giessen

Professor Dr. W. HAMM
University of Marburg
Germany

SUMMARY

1. <u>GENERAL CONSIDERATIONS</u>

1.1 THE PROBLEM

The economic situation of nearly all European railway under-takings has been unsatisfactory for many years and in some countries, especially the Federal Republic of Germany, it is alarming. Up to 8 per cent of the Federal German budget has to be spent on subsidising the Federal railways, which have become a financial risk.

Without embarking here on a systematic analysis of the reasons for this, mention will be made of the following main problems in railway policy:

- As income per head rises and private car ownership increases, the demand for passenger transport by rail decreases. This is especially true of short journeys in the open country (outside areas of industrial concentration), whereas in long-distance passenger transport it is quite possible for the railways, by raising the quality of their service, to hold their own, at least in terms of passenger kilometres.
- Likewise in freight transport the increasing demands of industrial customers for better quality and the rapid rise in the quantity and quality of road freight services are ousting the railways, especially from parcelled freight business and open-country routes.
- Changing patterns of production in different countries, such as a proportionate decline in raw materials industries and basic industries in favour of manufacturing industry, may specially handicap railway freight and favour road freight.
- In some European countries competition from inland water-ways has deprived the railways of considerable amounts of bulk freight, because water-borne services have noticeably improved the quality of their facilities and have been able to benefit from artificial cost advantages over the rail-ways thanks to indirect subsidies.
- Management of railways as State undertakings or as semi-government enterprises has seriously impaired the adapt-ability they need with regard to organisation, pricing, investment and personnel policy.

- Despite increasing competition in the passenger and freight
  transport markets, the railways have been used intensively
  as an instrument of the national, economic and social
  policies of governments and treated in almost the same way
  as in the twenties when they enjoyed a monopoly.
- As a rule genuine attempts at reforms for stabilizing the
  situation of the railways in the long term are only made
  when the need for subsidies from public funds becomes
  politically unacceptable. The resulting pressure to resort
  to short-term measures can then lead to erroneous decisions
  which attempt to remove only the symptoms and not the causes
  of the crisis.

1.2 FUTURE MODAL SPLIT IN SHORT AND LONG-DISTANCE TRANSPORT

1) In assessing the railways' future share of total passenger
and freight traffic the starting points are:

- the purposes of journeys and the travel connections which
  they require;
- the future pattern of freight transport as determined by
  the locations of industries and trade and by developments
  in particular sectors (and industries).

A distinction should be made between status quo forecasts which
project into the future the present patterns of transport services and
organisation and the present market behaviour of the railways, and
modified status quo forecasts which allow for structural changes in
technical and organisational potential.

It should be investigated whether and to what extent government
intervention in the process of allocating transport for future requirements can in general bring about substantial improvements in the
situation of the railways and in the supply of transport services.

2) Since the mid-fifties the main problem for the railways in
all developed economies has been that their organisation and services
structure have become increasingly out of line with customers' demands
for transport, while their competitors on the roads and to some extent
also on inland waterways have greatly strengthened their relative
position in the market.

This has not only led to a steady decline, reaching 50 per cent
in some countries, in railway freight traffic over more than 50 km
distances in terms both of tonnage (t) and of output (tkm). To a much
greater extent it is seen in a declining share of passenger traffic
(in both passengers carried and output). For example, the railways'
share of passenger traffic in the Federal Republic of Germany fell
from 37 per cent in 1950 to 6.5 per cent in 1975. Similar trends are

seen in the United Kingdom, Sweden, and the Netherlands (especially in
passenger traffic, because in that country freight traffic ranks very
low and since 1955 has actually fallen in absolute terms).

3) However, the unfavourable economic situation of railway undertakings is not only a result of the relative and absolute decrease in
their business. The patterns of services supplied, their organisational
principles and their workforces have not been adjusted to this trend,
but in many cases have been largely maintained as they were. Only in
a few countries (the United Kingdom, the Netherlands, France and
Sweden) were some partially successful attempts made in the fifties to
arrest the decline by making changes in the patterns of services and
organisational structures and in the relations between the railways
and the State. No striking success can be seen in the sense of loss-
free operation, although the extent of the economic crisis in the railways was reduced by these measures. In some countries (the Federal
Republic of Germany and Austria) new overall planning proposals were
not put forward until the mid-seventies and signs of their practical
implementation are not yet clearly visible.

4) In considering the railways' future prospects it should be
remembered that the starting point for freight transport is never more
than a derived demand so that traffic forecasts must be made for the
railways in each country and must estimate separate figures for each
main commodity group so as to arrive at total figures for freight
traffic in the future. Such forecasts will make assumptions regarding
the future pattern of the variables which determine the demand for
transport and these variables should be treated as basic socio-economic
factors independent of transport operations. The calculations will
include the interplay of domestic and international production and
trade flows (input-output relationships) and expected changes in
patterns of production and geographical location.

The next step it to assess future modal split in freight traffic
and here, apart from specific affinities of commodities for certain
modes of transport, assumptions must be made regarding the future
pattern of supply of transport services. In addition, allowance should
be made for possible measures of economic policy involving government
intervention in the supply of transport or influencing demand directly
or indirectly. However, one of the main factors determining future
modal split in freight traffic is the quantity and quality of the railways' transport potential, whose structure is multi-dimensional
(pattern of output, marketing system, organisational structure, network structure and actual market behaviour).

5) In the case of passenger traffic the basic magnitudes for the
forecast are population structure (age, size of families and types of
occupation), extent of car ownership, trend of social product, and
leisure statistics. Separate forecasts are desirable for population
groups which are distinguished by special travel behaviour.

It is also necessary to break down the forecast of future
mobility by purposes of travel, in particular:

- to and from work;
- weekend travel;
- holiday travel;
- business trips;
- other travel.

With the aid of the above basic social and economic data, which
are to be calculated separately, it is thus possible to forecast the
total amount of passenger traffic. In doing so, a plausible set of
assumptions should be worked out for the supply of transport (infrastructure, quality factors in the different modes, and price and cost
relationships in public and private transport). These assumptions
should take account of changes which are now visible in supply factors
and modify the status quo, but should otherwise presuppose a basically
unaltered structure of supplies of private and public transport.

The next step in estimating future modal split in passenger traffic must depend on the purposes of travel and will involve the trip-
distance structure. As the first distinction to make in modal split
is only between public and private transport, another approach can
consist in forecasting private car ownership and average mileage
driven per year. With the aid of passenger-kilometre figures weighted
by the expected average occupancy rate of private cars, a total
residual figure can be calculated by subtraction from total passenger
traffic and this will be distributed between the railways, other public short and long-distance passenger transport services and air
services.

6) All existing forecasts of railway freight traffic up to 1990
or 2000 point to absolute increases, but slight proportional decreases.
The main reason for this is that the special affinities between rail
transport and types of commodity are found in main commodity groups
whose transport requirements either increase very little or even
decrease as a result of structural changes in the pattern of production
and geographical distribution. This effect is called the commodity
structure effect. In addition, account must be taken of the substitution effect, which is a result of competition in quality of price
between modes of transport. The railways have to face strong
competition from internal waterways for bulk freight, especially in
the countries along the Rhine, but also in the Danube basin, as a
result of which there is a combination of the commodity structure
effect and the substitution effect. In almost all countries road
freight transport is displacing the railways in parcelled freight and
high-value wagon-loads, and to some extent also in container transport.

This should all be seen against the background of quite a low
transport elasticity in developed economies, i.e. total freight

traffic during the period of the forecast will grow more slowly than production and consumption (transport elasticity will be less than one).

7) The forecasts for the Federal Republic of Germany up to 1990 show rates of growth for the main commodity groups which are in some cases drastically lower than the rates between 1960 and 1972 (maximum annual average increases in chemicals, fertilizers and capital goods will be 4 per cent, while in most other commodities the estimated increase will be less than 1.5 per cent). In terms of the future distribution of traffic this means that railway freight traffic (in tkm) over long distances will fall by 1 per cent compared with 1972, while long-distance freight traffic by road will increase by 3 per cent (and over short distances by 4 per cent).

By virtue of the commodity structure effect, these forecasts mean that up to 1990 the average distances covered by internal water transport and pipeline transport will decrease, while those covered by road freight transport (both short and long-distance) will remain unchanged and those covered by rail freight transport will slightly increase. The change in modal split up to 1990 will be due mainly to the commodity structure effect and less to the substitution effect.

The results of these forecasts should be a valid indication of trends for other developed economies also. They mean that in future the railways must expect to carry freight which will increase in absolute terms, but at a very low rate, while their share of total freight traffic will fall. Meanwhile, road freight traffic will continue to expand strongly.

8) These forecasts depend on two important conditions being fulfilled.

- It is assumed that the railways will continue their past or present patterns of services, organisational principles and market behaviour but, as these factors together with continual government intervention in railway operating policy have greatly contributed to their underlying crisis, structural reforms and a new relationship between State and railways might put the latter on the road to improvement.
- The principle is recognised that the customer has the last word in the sense that industrial consignors should have a free choice of mode, but it should be mentioned that many proposals have been made and to some extent embodied in transport policy (e.g. in Sweden) for steering freight towards the railways by directly influencing the choice of mode.

Both these conditions will be discussed more fully later.

9) The forecasts for <u>passenger</u> traffic show that, compared with
the period from 1960 to 1972, future growth rates will be distinctly
lower because of the falling population recorded in some countries
and the decreasing number of journeys per inhabitant. On the other
hand, the average trip distance will increase, so that passenger-
kilometres will increase more than passenger numbers.

The railways' best prospects here lie in business and holiday
travel, whereas in commuting and recreational travel the private car
will keep its very high share of the traffic. For business travel the
air services will increase their competition as trip distances over
350 km increase, and the railways can meet it only by raising their
average speeds over distances up to 500 or 600 km and providing a
high degree of comfort.

It should be mentioned here that in some countries, especially
France, high speeds have already been achieved thanks to favourable
topographical conditions and route planning, relatively sparse populations between towns, and the location of dense populations and industrial concentrations in widely separated areas, as well as to a
high standard of technical performance. In most countries, however,
passenger train speeds are quite low (between 70 and 110 km/h over
long distances).

Private travel is greatly affected by subjective ideas regarding
costs and quality which lead to a strong preference for the private
car. In some countries, especially the Federal Republic of Germany,
however, passenger fares are now so high that the railway is no longer
competitive on financial grounds for family travel.

10) The forecasts make it clear that in the next 20 years in most
countries the position of the railways will not improve as regards
either the amount of freight or passenger traffic they carry or the
distances over which they carry it. Consequently their economic situation will further deteriorate, because they cannot offset the steady
increase in costs due to their labour-intensiveness by correspondingly
higher earnings. The gap between earnings from the market and costs
will become wider, unless it is possible

- to adapt the railways to future market requirements so as
  to maintain their share of traffic, and
- to reduce perceptibly the costs of providing railway
  services.

2. <u>DIAGNOSING THE CAUSES</u>

The most effective way of correcting misdirected trends is to diagnose their causes and treat them accordingly. It is therefore important to summarise the railways' main sources of loss. These come under five headings:

- The railways themselves point insistently to extensive intervention by government authorities which hampers management on businesslike lines, raises costs and restricts profits.
- In most European railways the productivity of the work-force increases considerably more slowly than in the economy as a whole and in competing transport undertakings. Many railways operate too expensively, especially because of high personnel costs.
- In many countries the range of railway services has not yet been well enough adjusted to the changed conditions of demand and competition. This again is to a large extent due to defective business management and to misallocation of functions and managerial responsibilities.
- In some ways the railways are handicapped in competing with other transport undertakings and in some countries they suffer from distortion of competition.
- There is considerable surplus capacity for maintaining and replacing vehicles and installations. In many countries undertakings which are run by a State railway monopoly and not given independence operate at comparatively high cost.

The following are explanatory comments on these five headings.

2.1 RELATIONSHIP BETWEEN GOVERNMENT AUTHORITIES AND RAILWAYS

The major State railway undertakings have always been exposed to extensive government influence, which is the result partly of their previous monopoly status and partly of government efforts to pursue various political aims by intervening in their business policy. Here regional and social policy aims deserve special mention. Government directives on tariff policies for passenger and freight services, the obligation to operate services and carry traffic, and directives on the details of the network and the remuneration of railway personnel have for long drastically restricted the scope for railway undertakings to manage themselves on businesslike lines on their own responsibility.

Many railways have also been handicapped by their dependence on the
State for supplies of investment capital for modernisation and
rationalisation.

2.2 UNDULY SLOW RISE IN PRODUCTIVITY

In nearly all railway undertakings the productivity of labour
increases considerably more slowly than wages and salaries, despite
continual additions of capital, with the result that they lose more
and more money. Several reasons, either alternative or cumulative,
can be given for this.

- On political grounds many railways have, at least temporarily,
  not raised their tariffs in line with market trends or they
  have tried by means of a deliberate low-tariff policy to
  attract additional traffic to the railways, usually with
  little success, because competitors have put up a good
  fight and the effectiveness of price as a marketing instrument is overestimated.

- In some countries, including the United Kingdom, too many
  persons are employed as a result of trade union pressure,
  and manpower reductions demanded by rationalisation are
  often not made or are seriously delayed. This could be a
  further reason why, despite heavy investment, many railways
  have not noticeably increased their productivity nor reduced
  their losses. Similar conditions to those in the United
  Kingdom have also been found in the Federal Republic of
  Germany (by the Bundesrechnungshof, i.e. the Federal Audit
  Office).

- There have been very few initiatives to switch to cheaper
  production methods and so increase labour productivity.
  Many railways are administered rather than managed on
  commercial lines and many exhibit a high degree of immobility
  despite radical changes in market data. This applies, for
  example, to using more buses in place of highly unprofitable railway passenger services over short distances outside
  population centres. According to the report by the German
  State Secretaries' Working Party on "Transport and Regional
  Policy" of February 1977, the Federal German Railways lose
  some DM 2.8 billion a year on these services alone (in
  1976 they required subsidies totalling DM 10.5 billion),
  whereas bus services require no or little subsidisation.

2.3 ADAPTING THE RANGE OF SERVICES

As mentioned at the beginning, the demand for transport services
has been changing significantly as a result of the rising standard of
living, customers' increasing demands, changing geographical distribution and patterns of production, and changing conditions of competition in transport markets, but to these changes many railways have
reacted mainly in a passive manner. The falling demand for railway
services has been only partly exploited for weeding out services which
have become unprofitable, while in many countries little use has been
made of opportunities for organising and supplying fast, punctual and
cheap services on trunk routes between major centres.

2.4 HANDICAPS DUE TO DISTORTED COMPETITION

Many railways complain that certain transport policy measures do
not affect all transport undertakings equally, but handicap the railways in competing with other modes. In this connection reference is
often made to the charges payable for using public highways, canals,
etc. and it would seem to be true, at least in countries which charge
low tolls, etc., that the railways are handicapped in competing by the
sometimes widely differing charges levied in different countries on
motor vehicles and inland shipping. Moreover, the railways are uni-
laterally handicapped in competing by other factors already mentioned,
e.g. controlled tariffs or bans on closing down sections of line. To
what extent these handicaps are offset by advantages, e.g. in taxation
or as a result of special government financial support or statutory
limits on the development of competing undertakings, could only be
discovered by making special investigations in each country.

2.5 UNECONOMIC STATE MONOPOLIES

Many railways supply services themselves which they could obtain
more cheaply from the market. These include a) the repair, maintenance
and construction of rolling stock and the maintenance and renewal of
track /see Section 4 (6)7, and b) railway-owned motor transport undertakings for passengers and freight which use vehicles belonging to the
railways.

Attempts are often made to show that auxiliary undertakings owned
by a State monopoly are economic by not debiting them with their share
of the inevitable overheads, the concealed aim of such attempts being
to preserve as many jobs in the railways as possible. The losses
from these undertakings are then debited to other sectors, where they
may lead to measures detrimental to one or more sectors of the economy.

The experiences of several railway undertakings show that considerable economies can be made by giving motor transport undertakings
an independent legal status and by procuring repair, maintenance and
replacement services from the market, the main reasons being a more
adaptable and stricter personnel policy and a more efficient utilisation of means of production.

Considerable savings can normally be achieved if railway undertakings, instead of using their own motor vehicles, hire buses and
lorries from private firms and have them driven by outsiders. In this
way, operating costs can be considerably reduced. In addition,
appreciable savings in administrative expenses should be possible by
giving independent legal status to motor transport undertakings owned
by State monopolies.

This list of reasons for the serious and ever-increasing losses
suffered by railway undertakings is certainly not exhaustive, but no
doubt includes all the main items. The following paragraphs will investigate in what ways one can at least freeze the losses and if
possible reduce substantially the need to subsidise railways.

3. OUTLOOK FOR THE FUTURE PATTERN OF RAILWAY SERVICES

The following paragraphs start by assuming that in choices of
transport mode the principle to remember is that the customer has the
last word, although in view of the critical situation of the railways
and increasing congestion on the roads many countries are trying to
raise the railways' utilisation factor by means of measures for
managing demand.

Almost all these attempts, however, focus on road freight transport, and demand management policies pay hardly any attention to
passenger transport by private cars, which is much more important in
quantitative terms. The main reason for this is probably the expected
massive resistance from motorists and its effects on the electorate.

The customer's key position in the transport market means freedom for the consignor to choose his mode of transport to suit his
ideas regarding price and quality. If his choice is to be the optimum
for the economy as a whole, the total costs incurred by a transport
undertaking in providing its services, i.e. operational, maintenance,
infrastructure and pollution costs, must be charged to the demand side.
As a general principle, the total social costs of providing a transport
service should not exceed its total social benefits, as otherwise the
overall economy would suffer a loss. The social costs and benefits
include the so-called external negative and positive effects. In the

case of transport there is the problem that it is not at present
possible to quantify these external effects completely, so that the
analyst has to work only with quantifiable costs and benefits.

If a transport undertaking such as a railway is unable to cover
its costs with its earnings from the market over a long period, it
will be in danger of making a negative contribution to public welfare.
This would happen unless there were in addition important other positive external effects and, if possible, no other negative effects.
The discussions on the extent of the positive and negative external
effects produced by various transport modes are not yet concluded, nor
can agreed views be found, so that this problem area will not be
tackled here. Instead it will be assumed that the positive and negative external effects of railways more or less balance each other out
(positive = the effects of opening up territory and creating a network, consuming energy and polluting the environment; negative = the
effects of cutting up land areas and disturbing the environment by
noise).

A long-standing steady or increasing operational deficit will
then mean that there is a negative contribution to public welfare
because customers are not prepared to purchase the services offered
at such prices and in such quantities that earnings would cover total
costs.

The task will thus be to reduce the costs of providing the services and to increase the earnings from them.

3.1 PASSENGER TRAFFIC

The following are the implications for passenger traffic.

1) In all European countries a further rise in car ownership is
to be expected in line with future income per head. This means that
the tendency to use private cars for excursions, holidays and commuting
will keep growing unless the railways take steps to stop it.

2) The rise in car ownership will increase mobility and lead to
demands for more comfortable public transport. Greater mobility will
make possible changes in population distribution such that new resi-
dential areas can be developed outside present conurbations. According
to past experience this will require the use of private cars, because
high-performance public transport cannot be regarded as normal and
when there are several workers in a family they can either share a car
or they have to use different transport modes because they go to
different work places.

Rail transport in the form of special high speed systems is
economic only for commuting from the outskirts of very large conurbations. In open country where there are no dense population centres,
commuter traffic should not be carried by rail on grounds of cost,

but by setting up regional transport organisations based on demand-oriented bus systems.

The future pattern of railway services will be dominated by mass traffic between major centres which will include both freight and passenger traffic. In a few special cases the services will be short-distance (up to 50 km), but they will mostly be long-distance. For short-distance passenger transport in open country the railways:

- are too expensive because they are labour-intensive in this class of transport, have relatively high additional operating and maintenance costs (safety requirements), and have a utilisation factor which varies greatly throughout the day so that its average is very low;
- have a standard of quality which cannot usually compete with the private car. Moreover, account must be taken of the greater elasticity of buses and the scope for raising the technical and organisational quality of bus systems above today's standard.

3) As regards business trips, the railways have an opening in trips between 250 and 500 kilometres. Strong competition comes from the private car over shorter distances and from air travel over longer ones. As here again the strongest competitor is the private car, the railways' strength lies in their <u>speed</u> and <u>travel comfort</u> and in their ability to schedule departures and arrivals at <u>convenient times</u> of day. In this case also the traffic in question is between <u>major centres</u>. Speeds should be over 140 km/h and shuttle services every two hours should be provided between centres with heavy traffic.

4) Holiday and recreational traffic will in general increase in the future insofar as income per head and the number of days' leave increase (second annual holiday and short holidays), but the railways will still be badly placed in the market.

- A considerable proportion of transfrontier holiday trips are made by air.
- Railway travel times to holiday destinations are often uncompetitive with car travel times because of the need to change trains and transfer baggage.
- On some West European railways the fare reductions now granted to families with children are not sufficient to attract them to rail travel. When they have a car, economic arguments point to using it for holiday trips, because the only costs considered are those connected with the trip, or often only the marginal costs. Thus the potential market for holiday and recreational travel by rail should shrink still further in future. It will come mainly from those customers who, because of

their age or because they have no car, cannot use private
transport or who are able to choose the comfortable trains
run for businessmen.

5) These unfavourable long-term prospects apply even more to
occasional trips and excursions, for which more use will be made in
future of the private car as a means of transport in the open country
and for long distances. The railway is competitive only between major
centres and these play little part in such traffic.

6) The conclusions for a policy for railway passenger traffic
point to the following requirements:

- increased efforts, by means of an investment policy and
  reorganisation, to raise speeds to at least 140 km/h on
  trunk services between major centres;
- improved travel comfort by modernising rolling stock
  (quieter running and air conditioning);
- introduction of regular frequency timetables;
- more car parks at stations for long-distance trains,
  as provided at airports;
- increased efforts to make rail travel financially
  attractive by means of special area and season tickets;
- improved service by making railway staff less bureaucratic
  in their attitudes;
- discontinuation of open-country services which are mainly
  used for commuting. These cost-intensive rail services
  should be replaced by customer-designed bus services.
  Whether rail freight services, which cost less because
  their quality and safety requirements are less, can hold
  their own on such subsidiary routes will depend on the
  particular freight situation on them;
- examination of the scope for providing further "car
  sleeper" services. In several countries experience with
  these services has not been satisfactory. The _railways_
  complain of:

  - undesirable bunching of bookings on a few dates;
  - problems in loading the cars;
  - failure to cover total costs in this branch of traffic;

  while _customers_ complain of:

  - difficulties in making reservations owing to the limited
    capacity provided;
  - problems and irregularities in loading vehicles;
  - excessive prices for the package of services (transport
    of vehicle and passengers including wagon-lit or couchette).

7) Where rail services in the open country are desirable on grounds of regional or social policy, the institutions which demand them should have to pay special compensation depending on the sections of line concerned.

8) The medium and long-term improvements required in the quality of passenger transport, especially higher speeds, demand investment in track and rolling stock. It should not become a rule that the most uneconomic sector of railway transport, i.e. short-distance passenger transport, should be given the technically most advanced and therefore very expensive vehicles and infrastructure. The impression that this is so is given by some high speed systems in the immediate catchment area of cities of over 500,000 inhabitants.

Instead, when allocating investment funds, a compromise should be found between investment in high speed rail transport and in medium and long-distance transport for business, holiday and occasional travel.

9) It should be ascertained to what extent investment schemes and to what extent organisational measures can help to separate freight traffic from passenger traffic on routes between major centres. In doing this allowance should be made for the possibility that the structure of railway passenger and freight services may be considerably altered.

In view of the shortage of funds and of the considerable financial burdens imposed by investment schemes, more importance than before must be given to the reorganisation made possible by unravelling traffic. The rebuilding of entire sections of line should be subjected to particular scrutiny because:

- some of the existing short-distance passenger trains serving both the open country and routes between major centres will disappear and be replaced by bus systems when the pattern of services is changed;
- the medium-term justification must also be queried for part of the short-distance rail freight network which in some countries is mainly used for hauling single wagons and distributing parcelled freight, so that the number of trains making frequent stops will fall;
- the introduction of regular frequency timetables for long-distance passenger services will make it easier to plan passenger and freight services jointly. It should be considered to what extent regular frequency timetables might also be introduced for fast freight trains so as to facilitate the scheduling of total traffic and also be able to guarantee goods wagon journey times.

10) By changing the pattern of rail services one could achieve
a largely uniform standard in the passenger and freight services provided. There would be more scope for organisational measures for improving output and trains could be speeded up.

On the other hand, investment is necessary when the track or
signalling are inadequate for **higher** speeds and when engineering work
is required for straightening sections of line.

Track should only be completely rebuilt after making detailed
calculations of profitability in the light of operational and general
economic considerations. It should be a condition that such investment schemes should ultimately be financed from the higher returns
they yield and that public funds should be used only for pre-financing.

3.2 FREIGHT TRAFFIC

3.2.1 Reasons for the railways' shrinking share of the market

In the last three decades the railways' share of the freight
market has fallen considerably in all ECMT countries. There are
several reasons for this:

- changes in the structure of demand, especially the continuing decrease in the transport of base materials and
  the fast growing transport of high-value commodities with
  usually low specific weights in small consignments;
  owing to the increasing division of labour this change in
  demand structure will continue in future;
- large-scale road development; modern fast roads have done
  much to shorten the turn-round times of lorries and riase
  the productivity of lorry drivers;
- competition between road carriers and between inland
  waterway carriers with resulting increases in efficiency;
- expansion of transport by pipeline; and
- the small extent to which many railways adjust to the
  new market conditions.

Compared with road transport, the railways can carry heavy traffic between a limited number of stations at unbeatably low prices,
yet consignments filling entire trains and large groups of wagons are
becoming fewer. However, the special advantages of rail freight could
also be obtained by despatching in wagon loads, if the organisational
and operational requirements were met, i.e. the ability to satisfy
differing customer demands (for many single wagon loads between
different starting points and destinations) by means of a standardised
operating system. As a rule, medium and long-distance consignments
of small size can be bunched on a section of line with no expensive

single handling of wagons (collecting single wagons at numerous small
stations, attaching them to long-distance goods trains, often several
time-consuming rearrangements during the journey, and distribution
between stations of destination with the aid of short-distance goods
trains) and can be taken to near their destination with hardly any
expensive shunting operations. Admittedly efforts to standardise
rail freight services by minimising expensive collecting and distribution operations by rail would be a break with traditional methods,
but they would create new openings for the railways in sectors of the
freight market which are now regarded as lost to them. The necessary
conditions for this will have to be considered further.

By strictly limiting their freight services to heavy traffic and
bunched consignments between major centres the railways would overcome
a second handicap vis-à-vis road freight, namely their unduly slow
service. In general, the railways are at present far behind their
competitors in making freight space available punctually, in transit
times and in keeping to schedule. As for many consignors transit
times are a decisive factor in choosing a mode of transport, substantially shortening them, as is quite feasible, should evoke positive
reactions from customers.

3.2.2 <u>Limitation to trunk routes</u>

1) It is comparatively expensive for a railway system to serve
numerous small stations and works sidings with little traffic and one
of the main reasons for the low productivity of labour and capital in
railways is that in many countries they keep providing widely differing services for different areas. Small short-distance goods trains
which run slowly and stop often, frequent shunting operations and
moving single wagons to and from works sidings keep the productivity
of labour and capital in the railways at a low level. Compared with
other types of traffic the distances covered by the wagons and locomotives are very small. Weeding the list of loading and unloading
points for railway freight should therefore be judged not only by the
number of staff who can be economised at the goods stations to be
closed down. Much more important are the indirect effects on labour
and capital productivity which, however, will only become visible
when - assuming an unchanged level of traffic - redundant personnel
and superfluous locomotives, wagons and fixed installations of various
kinds have in fact been economised. Because in many countries railway
personnel cannot in practice be dismissed and because of the long
economic life of capital equipment, perceptible savings will only be
achieved by a foresighted policy for staffing and disinvestment.

2) The technical problem of bunching railway freight is not found
when running complete trains or running groups of wagons between works
sidings. In the case of bulk freight which is concentrated only at

the point of departure or arrival (single-ended dispersion) and in the
case of heavy traffic in non-bulk freight the question arises how the
railways can avoid the highly expensive process of collecting or distributing numerous small consignments by rail. This cannot be done
quickly and radically, but only in many separate stages by enlisting
the use of road vehicles, preferably in close co-operation with
specialised road carriers. It is recommended first to close down
specially expensive services to and from small freight forwarding
offices and works sidings, while making rail transport between major
centres attractive by providing faster and cheaper services. Here it
is of prime importance to lower loading and unloading costs (by
choosing simple and rapid handling systems). Owing to the fast growth
in international freight traffic it is urgent to reach agreement on
internationally standardised loading units and handling systems.

As regards organisation, several solutions can be envisaged. The
railways can provide transport in complete trains between major centres
for own or customer's account. In the latter case the risk of un-
utilised capacity would be borne by specialist undertakings which
would buy complete trains and be responsible for filling them. In
the former case the railways themselves (as the carriers) would make
contracts with consignors and would be responsible for making the best
use of the capacity provided. Examples of the second arrangement are
the British freightliner system and the German Kombiverkehrs KG.

3) The fear is often expressed that closing down small goods
stations and works sidings may lead to loss of traffic for the railways, but this fear is unfounded if the railways' tariffs demonstrate
their cheaper costs in carrying heavy traffic when suitably organised,
and if they ensure that loading and unloading at stations in major centres
are fast and cheap. For short distances the preference will admittedly
be given to direct raod transport, but it should be remembered that
the railways also carry additional traffic which helps to worsen their
trading results (the additional receipts are less than the additional
costs in the short term and even more so in the long term).

A report by the Federal German Minister of Transport and Communications for 1976 states that "in general the railways are producing
too much too expensively and often in the wrong place", and this
criticism probably applies in varying degrees to most other European
railways. Apart from reducing staff, the remedy is to be found in
improving efficiency in the railways' particular markets by concentration and investment. The Federal German Railways have calculated that
with a system of freight services for major centres (which is still far
from reality), it would be possibe to make up considerably more single-
destination long-distance goods trains and so greatly shorten transit
times; 70 per cent of all wagon loads could then reach their destination within 16 hours and a further 20 per cent within 36 hours.

However, whether these measures would suffice to arrest the decline
in freight traffic and raise productivity sufficiently is doubtful
and in all probability further steps in the same direction will have
to be taken.

3.2.3 Capacity management policy

1) Capacity management policy has an important bearing on trading
results from railway freight operations. Experience shows that in
many countries rolling stock capacity for carrying freight is over-
generous and in this connection the need is often mentioned to be able
to deal smoothly with peak traffic.

Surplus capacity not only causes avoidable expenditure, but is
also a temptation to make use of idle capacity by granting price con-
cessions. Even where such price reductions can be prevented from
having direct repercussions on other railway operations (demands from
other customers for similar favourable tariffs), the railways' price
level will usually come under pressure. The aim of concessionary
freight rates is almost always to win business from competitors. If
the policy succeeds, the undertakings hit by it must be expected to
follow similar policies in other markets with adverse results for the
railways' load factor. Surplus capacity is a major cause of the poor
earnings of many transport undertakings.

2) Seasonal price differentiation would be a way of flattening
peaks in demand. To some extent demand would be shifted to periods
when capacity was less utilised and this would help to steady the load
factor. The more inflexible the price structure, the more marked are
the peaks in demand.

The view is often expressed that seasonal variations in freight
rates would be an unsuitable means for shifting freight orders to
periods before or after traffic peaks. Where such seasonal conditions
are found, transport undertakings could raise their prices so high
during peak demand that the costs of reserving capacity for peak periods
could be fully covered. There is no reason, for example, why the taxpayer should bear the financial consequences of surplus capacity
alleged to be required for dealing with peak traffic.

3) Many railways are still far from taking full advantage of
opportunities for utilising their capacity better and this applies
especially to rolling stock. Before capacity is increased a careful
check should therefore be made whether all the avenues have been ex-
plored for increasing turn-round speeds and shortening unproductive
idling times of locomotives and goods wagons. If big customers of the
railways are encouraged to purchase their own wagons (private wagons),
the railways' investment risk can be reduced.

4) In addition, the capacity of fixed installations must change
with changes in demand, which admittedly raises considerable difficulties in view of the long life of these investment goods and the

time required for constructing new installations. Owing to the
heavy investment cost of additional railway infrastructure, plans
for new construction should be scrutinised very carefully. The capacity of bottlenecks can be increased by smoothing the flow of traffic (running goods and passenger trains at similar speeds), by serving
small intermediate stations by road and by modernising the signalling.
Thought should also be given to diverting goods traffic to less
crowded lines. If these measures are not sufficient to deal with the
traffic, the first step is to consider giving up unprofitable traffic.
Investment in extensions should only be made when all possibilities
have been exhausted of making better use of existing capacity and it
still seems likely that new sections of line would yield an economic
return (benefit-cost ratio) in the foreseeable future.

3.2.4 Reducing costs by investment

Losses on freight traffic can be reduced not only by economies
in personnel and by making technical and organisational changes.
The productivity of labour could also be increased by investment in
rationalisation and modernisation. Among other things this means investing in modern goods wagons with a greater payload (up to 100 t),
technical innovations which reduce loading and unloading costs, re-
inforcing the track, and electronic traffic control systems. On the
other hand, the introduction of automatic couplings is rightly no
longer discussed. According to recent calculations the costs of this
investment bear no relation to the benefits obtainable from it, especially if the number of shunting operations is drastically reduced
by concentrating on traffic between major centres. In the extreme
case of complete trains on shuttle services, automatic coupling is
hardly any advantage. The number of operations in making up trains
and of rearrangement operations during journeys can also be reduced
by efforts to achieve uniform operation. Consequently earlier esti-
mates of the profitability of automatic couplings must be regarded as
out of date.

3.2.5 Special problems of parcelled freight traffic

Forwarding small consignments separately by rail involves especially high costs. Although the Federal German Railways have
reduced the number of freight forwarding offices to 400 and although
they have reduced trans-shipment operations and improved their load
factor, they suffer heavy loss from their constantly diminishing
traffic and the switching of freight to the joint-cargo facilities
of road carriers. Many other railways providing comparable services
are in a similar situation.

The fact that road carriers can transport parcelled freight at a
profit or at least without loss (including collecting and distributing
it), while all railways suffer heavy losses on their parcelled freight
traffic means that they should further reduce parcelled freight operations and gradually phase them out. Where they succeeded in providing attractive rail services between major centres, they might win
back at least a part of this traffic in the form of grouped load operations.

Some railways point out that parcelled freight still makes a
small contribution to covering their overheads, so that giving it up
would further worsen their overall trading results. Here the following considerations apply:

- Every rise in wages hits the railways' parcelled freight
  operations very hard, because they involve unusually high
  personnel costs. As labour productivity in these operations increases much more slowly than wages, the time
  will come when they will no longer cover their costs, so
  the railways should adopt a foresighted policy.

- A short-term view would suggest that the great majority
  of overheads are independent of the amount of traffic and
  cannot be reduced. The nearer the planning horizon, the
  larger the contribution seems to be which parcelled
  freight traffic makes towards covering overheads. However, decisions whether to continue this traffic in its
  present form should be based on a longer-term analysis
  of the trends of costs and earnings. In the long term
  the proportion of costs to be economised will increase
  considerably, while cost-covering contributions will fall
  off or become negative.

There is much to be said for progressively reducing parcelled
freigh traffic in its present form and gradually phasing it out. In
this way the overall trading results from freight operations might be
improved in the medium term (see Section 7).

3.2.6 <u>Marketing policy guidelines</u>

Empirical tests show that in choosing transport modes for freight,
the overriding factors to be considered are freight rates, incidental
costs (e.g. packing), transit times, punctuality and safety (low
damage frequency). These criteria vary in importance with the type
of freight. Almost everywhere the railways still have considerable
scope for making themselves more attractive to customers and at the
same time improving their earnings from freight carried by purely
railway services.

Improved production techniques and organisation (by concentrating
on heavily-trafficked lines which avoid much shunting and making up of
trains) would make it possible:

1. To guarantee availability of wagons; comparable facilities
   are largely a matter of course in competing modes.
2. To promise that stated forwarding times will not be ex-
   ceeded.
3. To shorten forwarding times considerably; the aim would
   be whenever possible to get wagons to their destination
   by the morning following delivery of consignments ("night
   hop").
4. To reduce substantially the damage in transit (as a
   result of fewer shunting operations).
5. To economise in packing when shunting could be entirely
   dispensed with.

The railways could meet demands for "punctuality", "safety",
"short forwarding times" and "low additional forwarding costs" much
better than they can with their traditional methods.

The higher quality of service would enable the railways to improve their profitability by earning more. The fact that the rates for
long-distance freight by road are often higher than by rail shows that
customers are prepared to pay for a better quality of service.

Little success may be expected from a pricing policy of under-
cutting competitors without also improving service. Experience shows
that in transporting semi-manufactured and manufactured goods price is
less decisive than other factors. In this branch of traffic the price
elasticity of demand is obviously low and bringing down rates normally
leads to reduced earnings, which again makes clear the overriding importance of new techniques in rail transport.

An active marketing policy also includes detailed market studies
to see what freight which is not yet carried by rail would suit the
railways and could form part of complete trainloads. Such freight
could be won for the railways if suitable measures were taken. In
other words, marketing strategies should aim at changing to new techniques so as to alter the split between rail and road, driving away
traffic suitable for road transport and attracting traffic to the
railways which suited them. This marketing policy is not only desirable
from the point of view of the railways (improved earnings), but also on
general economic grounds (reduced cost of transport to the national
economy).

3.2.7 The network concept in railway systems

Some European countries whose railway network was constructed
mainly in the 19th century had adapted it by the middle of the 20th

century to the changed conditions of competition in transport markets, but other countries including the Federal Republic of Germany have still to do almost all of this work. Studies of branch lines have shown that of the total freight traffic in the areas concerned, only a few per cent is carried by rail, all the rest having long since switched to road transport. As regards transit times and frequency of service, the railways are hopelessly outclassed by road transport in the open country (quite apart from transport costs). Consignors have drawn their own conclusions from this.

Nevertheless there are cases where it seems justified to maintain a reduced service, at least during a transitional period. Sometimes traffic is still carried by branch lines because certain immobile consignors (sources of raw materials) regularly deliver large loads for despatch in groups of wagons. In such cases one might consider changing the branch lines into "lengthened sidings". Only when considerable investment in replacement became necessary would it have to be decided whether such rail traffic should be continued, having regard to its costs and benefits to the national economy.

In some countries, there are considerable difficulties in the way of rationalising the railway network, because people insist on the railways' obligation to run services and carry passengers and freight. For closing down a section of line or freight forwarding office there is an elaborate time-consuming approval procedure, even when the railways are prepared to provide equivalent transport services by road. It seems urgent to amend these legal regulations which prevent overdue structural adjustments from being made. The railways should be free to choose whether they will meet the operating and carrying obligations imposed on them by providing rail or road services. It would be quite easy to check whether these changed obligations were being fulfilled. Nor could any objection be made to altering the railways' obligations in this way on grounds of regional policy. Should government authorities nevertheless insist on continued services on unprofitable sections, special compensation payments from tax revenues should be provided for (see Section 5).

The operating and carrying obligation (public service obligation) is a relic from the time when the railways had a monopoly in many transport markets, but since the advent of the motor vehicle market conditions have changed so profoundly that this obligation has become superfluous wherever the railways fix their tariffs as they like. An obligation to do lucrative business is not a burden which need be imposed by the State.

3.2.8 <u>Hiving off specific transport functions</u>

Some railway services are abnormally expensive, which is due both to the size and unwieldiness of railway undertakings and to trade union influences and special government-imposed burdens on the railways. For example, it has been found that private carriers' lorries and buses run on behalf of the railways and under their direction have considerably lower operating, maintenance and management costs than the railways' own vehicles.

So it is clear that more use should be made of opportunities for having transport services provided by private undertakings on behalf of the railways. In other cases there is the possibility of delegating specific functions to subsidiary undertakings (e.g. workshops) and obliging the latter to cover their costs in competition with other undertakings. By this means overstaffing in these sectors could probably be cured more quickly and thoroughly than if the latter were not treated separately.

3.2.9 Conclusions for railway policy

Efforts to reduce the railways' losses on freight traffic should concentrate on the following points:

- cutting down unnecessary staff;
- concentrating on heavily-trafficked lines;
- thereby shortening transit times, raising the productivity of labour and capital; and
- drastically reducing shunting operations (with favourable effects on the level of damage in transit);
- giving up open-country services except in the case of heavy traffic from particular consignors who can remain connected via lengthened sidings;
- increasing the attractions of traffic between major centres by suitable marketing measures;
- avoiding surplus capacity;
- introduction of pricing policy measures for flattening traffic peaks;
- exploiting all means of improving load factors before investing in extensions (including smoothing the taffic flow through bottlenecks);
- investing in schemes for raising productivity, modernising and rationalising;
- medium and long-term strategies for phasing out persistently unprofitable freight services (especially parcelled freight);
- relaxing pricing requirements and carrier obligations;
- hiving off certain services which can be provided more cheaply by independent undertakings.

4. ORGANISATIONAL MEASURES

1) The intensive competition to which the railways are exposed
in almost all branches of freight and passenger taffic makes it all
the more urgent to consider what organisational arrangements are required for making their services and marketing more effective.

The primary aim must be to make all railway departments more
market-oriented, but as this can hardly be done in an enterprise
which is structured like a public service and managed like a government department, the railways must move further towards acting like
business enterprises. For this purpose the personnel must have more
individual responsibility, results must be monitored and more importance attached to the principle of performance.

2) The continuous monitoring of results means first that a railway undertaking must have a suitable accounting (costing) system for
recording and evaluating the separate out-turns in the different
branches of business. As well as recording full costs, there should
certainly be a direct costing system and it should be arranged that
business decisions on market policy and expenditure are taken in line
with the established figures for the trading results of each branch.
In particular a railway must be prepared to give up traditional
classes of operation in which it is no longer competitive because of
its technology and competition from other modes of transport.

3) Railways should adopt the profit-centre principle whereby each
undertaking is divided up into units which are responsible for their
own earnings and costs. The managers of these profit-centres must
be given the necessary freedom of decision on personnel and other
operational questions. One should also try to give the staff a share
in the profits so as to increase their incentive to reduce costs and/
or look for more business.

4) In this connection one should find out to what extent the
requirements of market-oriented management are met by a public-service
status, when one is still applied. In countries where railway staff
are still civil servants it will hardly be possible in the short and
medium term to change them over to private-enterprise status, but the
following aims should be pursued.

- In the medium and long term the railways should be given
  private-enterprise status instead of public-service status.
  Whether they should then be reconstituted under private
  law, and if so in what form, is a secondary question, the
  important point being to escape the inflexibility imposed
  by public-service status which has very damaging effects
  on railways.

- Meanwhile, in the short term full use should be made of
  the openings in the railways' public-service status for
  promoting their interests. In some countries this status
  has been narrowed by special agreements between railway
  trade unions and management, with the result that the
  railways and ultimately the taxpayer are overburdened and
  that public-service status lacks uniformity in practice
  because there are special arrangements for the railways.
  In such cases efforts should definitely be made to rescind
  the special conditions in the railways' public-service
  status which particularly handicap railway policy.

5) Many railway companies still suffer from a disproportion
between administrative and operational personnel. Thinking too much
in traditional terms and the rigidity of public-service status are
the reasons why there is often reluctance to scale down operationally
superfluous directorates and superintending bodies. The main criterion for determining the administrative structure of a railway
undertaking should always be the effectiveness of its management and
the attention which its production and sales policy pays to the market.

6) From long tradition and in order to create jobs many railway
companies have taken on operations which should now be checked for
profitability, mainly large-scale repair shops (especially for over-
hauling rolling stock), plants for building their own wagons, and
track maintenance services. It should be ascertained whether many
of these operations could not be performed by private enterprise at
less cost to the railways. The relevant calculations should assume
from the start that the personnel released by the new arrangements
would in fact cease to be employed by the railways and the next step
would be to find out what alternative employment there was for this
personnel, if in practice they could not be dismissed.

The labour-intensive nature of many railway undertakings and ultimately the main cause of the railways' plight are largely due to the
numerous enterprises they run which contribute only indirectly to providing railway service.

5. REGULATING RELATIONS BETWEEN STATE AND RAILWAYS

In the past, government authorities in many countries have in-
tervened in railway management for a wide variety of purposes (see
Section 2.1). Responsibilities were not clearly defined, so that the
blame for the railways' growing deficits cannot be clearly apportioned.

1) It would be possible to change this unsatisfactory state of
affairs, if on principle the railways only provided services which
paid their way. Where it seemed desirable for general economic or
policy reasons to provide more services than that, the railways would
have to be instructed accordingly by the competent government authorities. At the same time, special financial compensation payable by
the instructing authority would have to be stipulated, sufficient to
offset the resulting charge on the railways. Such an arrangement
would have the following advantages:

- Responsibilities would be clearly allocated between
  government authorities and railway undertakings, and the
  blame for the railways' large deficits could not be
  bandied arbitrarily between railway administrations and
  government departments.
- Instead of lumping together all the losses to be offset and
  so discouraging efforts to stop growing deficits and uneconomic management, governments would pay compensation to
  be agreed separately in each case and checked in the light
  of competitors' prices. If, for example, an unprofitable
  branch line was not closed down, it would be ascertained
  whether the railways' demand for compensation was in
  proportion to the general economic benefit and subsidisation involved in having a comparable service provided by other carriers.
- The payment of special compensation by an authority which
  considered uneconomic railway services to be necessary
  would act as a brake on demands for railway services which
  did not pay their way. In some countries today central
  government or local authorities who are not responsible
  for the railways' losses ask for unprofitable services to
  be continued at the expense of other government departments, with the result that the requests for loss-making
  railway services are excessive and there is no effective
  limit on calls for subsidisation.
- Railway administrations, although not under parliamentary
  control, have often decided policy aims on their own,
  which have then been pursued by means of loss-making railway services, or sometimes policy aims have been sought
  and found afterwards for services which have become unprofitable, thereby enabling the railways to evade the
  obligation to pay their way and adjust to changing market
  conditions.
- Scarce tax revenue can be spent in widely varying ways and
  so achieve different levels of political advantage. Railway administrations are not able to compare the political

benefits obtainable from alternative kinds of expenditure,
because they do not know the order of priority of political
aims and cannot compare their benefits. It is therefore
desirable for the political authorities to lay down binding
objectives, as only the responsible politicians concerned
can assess the opportunity costs.

2) A clear definition of functions and financial responsibilities
is only one aspect of the reform required in the relations between
railways and government authorities. In addition, the organisational
requirements must be met for efficient management (see Section 4).

3) Furthermore, the owners of railways should take more care
than before that they have enough own capital and outside capital.
In many countries they have for long not done so, with the result
that some railways could not take sufficient advantage of technical
progress, expensive bottlenecks arose and opportunities for rationalisation could not be fully exploited. Many countries have failed to
realise that timely investment could have prevented later losses.

Indeed past experience shows that it is essential to investigate
carefully whether the railways' earnings situation can really be improved by planned investment. Before an investment scheme is started,
one must be sure that the expected staff economies and productivity
increases can really be achieved, after which the results should be
monitored to see whether the calculations were correct. In addition
the right conclusions must be drawn, including those concerning
staffing, in case major investment schemes do not produce the results
claimed for them.

6. PROBLEMS OF POLITICAL AND ECONOMIC FEASIBILITY

1) In many countries one reason for the serious economic crisis
in the railways is that there are political and also some economic
difficulties in carrying out the proposals for solving or at least
defusing the problems, and it must be added that these difficulties
have kept increasing with time.

2) In the highly developed economies in the late fifties one
could already see the increasing gap between the supply of railway
services and the trends of demand, but at the time it was also recognised that there were considerable political difficulties in reshaping
railway policy. Every structural reform must inevitably involve discontinuing some traditional types of service and also lead to a perceptible reduction in personnel. As trade union influence on the

State railways' management policy has always been considerable and as there are often special trade unions for railway workers, they are naturally interested in keeping up the numbers of railway employees and therefore their membership as far as possible.

As long as the political authorities thought they could carry the economic risk of delaying or avoiding reforms in railway policy, they refrained from making real changes in it.

3) As the railways' economic difficulties increased, as shown mainly by the steadily increasing government payments for subsidising special public service obligations and financing annual deficits, the pressure from finance policy for structural reforms increased. Meanwhile, the extent of the necessary reforms kept increasing also, because the gap had kept widening in the transport market between the pattern of railway services and customers' requirements. The result was that the measures required to change the pattern of services and organisational structure in many countries are now very painful where planning is only on a short-term basis. The adjustment and re-structuring processes which the railways have delayed for years have become most urgent and much more extensive intervention is now required, which makes it difficult to take the necessary action.

In several countries the result of this situation is that certain groups demand:

- that at first caution should be exercised in making changes to suit the market, lest the traditional pattern of railway services be watered down;
- that policy should focus more on the railways' competitors, especially road freight transport, thereby largely exempting the railways from structural reforms because they are a public asset and deserving of protection.

4) In some countries and in some pressure groups there is a clear tendency to replace structural reforms for the railways by restrictive measures against road freight transport so as to ensure a better load factor for rail freight transport. Especially in Sweden, Austria and the Federal Republic of Germany it is almost traditional for the public to receive such a policy with sympathy. Attempts are usually made to justify the drastic limitation of consumer preference which this involves by claiming that it is nonsense to expect railways to pay their way. The argument runs that the railways provide all kinds of social benefits which do not appear in economic calculations and that competing modes of transport, especially road transport, involve social costs (pollution and a distorted allocation of expenditure on roads) which are not brought to account.

This argument, however, overlooks the following facts:

- In recent railway policy discussions the demand has
  never been seriously made that the railways should pay
  their way in the sense of continuously balancing their
  earnings and expenditure. The point is rather to
  stabilize their economic situation so that the expenditure of public funds on them will be brought down to a
  lower level. At the same time and as a priority, they
  should make a contribution to the general economy by
  at least balancing the total social benefits they provide
  with their total social costs. It must also be remembered
  that the large transfers of public funds required for
  maintaining the railways have to be deducted from some
  other head in the national accounts, which means that the
  annual costs to the overall economy of running the railways by increasingly subsidising them with funds from
  the national budget should be assessed as opportunity
  costs (should be given the value of the benefits lost by
  spending the funds in other ways). By this method of
  calculation the value of many European railways to the
  overall economy might well turn out to be even lower.
- The social benefits provided by the railways'
  competitors, especially road freight transport, are
  usually overlooked, as are the considerable social
  costs of the railways (noise and dividing up land).
  There is an absence of systematic reasoning based on
  overall economic magnitudes, so that there is no
  decisive argument against the demand for structural
  reforms in the railways.

In this connection one should consider separately requests to
eliminate the artificial distortion of competition between rival
modes. The important points here would seem to be the question of
road costing (especially in relation to inland waterways) and the
political toleration of individual management strategies followed by
railways. Continual government intervention in the railways'
business policies does much damage to their competitive position even
when they are paid compensation from public funds for running services on political grounds.

5) After the oil crisis in the autumn of 1973 the problems of
structural unemployment became much more serious in many European
countries and this had direct effects on railway policy.

Whereas some years ago, when workers were made redundant by
structural alterations in the production programme and by organisational measures, it was possible in many countries to transfer them
to non-railway jobs without seriously upsetting the labour market,

public services are regarded as being under a special social obligation to preserve jobs both now and in the foreseeable future. Thus owing to hesitation in transport policy an opportunity in the past was lost.

It is not possible by ruthlessly stopping recruitment to adjust the size of the railways' workforce to actual requirements when all rationalisation measures have been adopted. Apart from raising the average age, there would be the danger of producing a wrong quality structure, as the railways' changed job requirements would call for the recruitment and training of suitably qualified and specialised personnel.

Thus the relatively high rate of unemployment in the developed economies means that for political reasons possible adjustments in personnel cannot all be made. In the case of the Federal German Railways, conservative calculations indicate that by 1985 at least 30,000 employees will be redundant, but not dismissible, although recruitment will be drastically reduced so that the workforce will fall by some 60,000 persons (compared with 1974).

6) The function of railway services involves the necessity of providing replacement services and these will have to be found mainly in road passenger transport for short journeys in open country and in road freight transport in open country. Depending on the changes in the pattern of railway services, it will then be necessary to close down certain sections of the railway network which originated in historical circumstances.

Experience shows that this partial switching from rail traffic to road traffic leads to strong protests from regional institutions. While the latter want to remain connected to the railway system, they are usually not prepared to provide the sections concerned with adequate traffic or make special payments to the railways to finance their deficit.

7) To transform a railway into a market-oriented competitive transport undertaking requires not only concentration on certain types of service, but also the availability of investment funds. These funds are needed to enable the railway to strengthen its market position by improving both its infrastructure and its rolling stock.

In several countries the need for such funds has accumulated because in the last twenty years it has hardly been possible to maintain assets by making the necessary investment. The deficit position of a steadily increasing number of railway undertakings has inevitably helped to reduce investment funds in favour of current expenditure designed to cover losses.

In view of the severe strains on national budgets in all countries whose railways are in a critical position, it would seem to be difficult to provide the necessary investment capital in practice.

If it is possible at all, one must expect funds to be diverted from
investment in other transport sectors, especially from budgets for
road making, in favour of the railways. This will encounter resistance from road transport interests, so that ultimately here again
only compromise solutions are feasible whose aims have little connection with the productivity of the economy as a whole.

8) A rational railway policy and especially a rational restructuring policy require clear policy aims to be laid down together with
operational arrangements which make it possible to check whether they
are being fulfilled or not and to find the reasons for any failure to
fulfil them.

Experience shows that when the political institutions formulate
such aims, the process is difficult and protracted, which gives the
impression that they sometimes deliberately neglect the task of for-
mulating them so as to be able to keep using the railways as an instrument for many other purposes.

7. SUMMARY OF PROPOSALS AND IMPLEMENTING MEASURES

The difficult economic situation of most railways in European
countries requires short and medium-term measures, but these should
be embedded in a long-term plan for the railways. The following
points are of particular importance in a short and medium-term
stabilisation policy.

1) The main starting point for all plans for reform is the
market's future demands on the railways and the technical and economic
possibilities of satisfying them. The pattern of passenger and freight
services must be changed to suit market conditions and the railways'
cost structure. The age when the railways were a universal transport
undertaking handling every conceivable transport operation came to an
end more than 20 years ago. The requirements for overcoming the
crisis in the railways are adjustment to market conditions and cost-
consciousness.

2) In passenger traffic the railways' chances as undertakings
transporting by rail lie in high-grade business travel and to some
extent in holiday and occasional travel. For successful marketing
they must raise their speeds to 140-180 km/h, improve travelling comfort and introduce regular frequency timetables on important inter-city
links. For family travel and also for business travel more fare reductions should be granted for long distances and passenger numbers,
because in these cases travellers are very price-conscious and real
incentives can be effective.

Short-distance passenger traffic which is heavily concentrated within a few hours per day, especially because of commuters and trainees, can only be carried by rail if it is heavily subsidised. Here the solution is to divert open-country traffic from the railways to a good quality bus sytem. This arrangement would at the same time smooth out the flow of railway traffic so that medium and long-distance trains could be run at regular frequencies.

3) To achieve the big rise in productivity required by freight traffic one must make radical changes in the supply of railway services in the direction of more uniform operations but, if only because of the staff reductions involved, it would take a long time to make the associated adjustments. Another point is that existing installations must be used so long as earnings are enough to help to cover costs. In these circumstances it may take a long time to close down small freight forwarding offices on main lines and discontinue complete branch lines. Simplified goods train operations on branch lines involve relatively low maintenance costs. The first step would be to stop all investment in replacements and extensions for installations threatened with closing down, after which separate investigations would provide the evidence for deciding the date when individual installations ought to be closed down. New investment in rolling stock should be scrutinised particularly strictly, because rising turn-round speeds have the effect of increasing capacity. Specially vigorous efforts should be made to cheapen and speed up loading and unloading between railway and road vehicles and to introduce internationally standardised practices. Meanwhile marketing policy should concentrate on opening customer's eyes to the many advantages of a faster, cheaper and safer freight service between major centres.

4) In parcelled freight traffic with its abnormally high personnel costs the railways are inferior to specialised forwarding firms, so that appropriate measures for discontinuing their parcelled freight business are inescapable. Here again one should start by stopping investment and recruitment, after which stations handling little annual traffic should be closed down progressively. Meanwhile greater efforts should be made to attract the heavy traffic in group loads between major centres to the railways. In this connection thought should also be given to combined traffic using swap bodies, semi-trailers, saddle loaders and tractor-trailer units.

5) The proposed changes in the pattern of services would lead to considerable shifts in investment policy. Investment in replacements for subsidiary operations would have to cease and the rising productivity of capital equipment especially rolling stock, would likewise make investment in replacements and new equipment to some extent superfluous. A careful check should also be kept on new investment in track with its high costs. As restructuring proceeded, bottlenecks would come under

less presure; meanwhile there are still unused opportunities for increasing capacity (smoothing the flow of traffic, bigger payloads for
goods wagons and goods trains, improved signalling technique and automation). The investment funds so released, together with additional
funds, should be spent on making suitable use of technical progress -
synchronised with any possible reductions in personnel - for improving
the quality of passenger and freight services and achieving the
smoothest possible co-operation with short-distance road freight services. The necessary funds should be made available, because failure
to carry out urgent railway investment projects today must involve
much greater additional loss and budget expenditure tomorrow.

6) The key to every plan for stabilising the economic situation
of the railways is to reduce staff requirements whilst raising the
productivity of labour. This can be done by changing the pattern of
railway services (production programme) and adapting their business
organisation to the changed production programme. In particular more
use should be made of opportunities for automation on the railways,
which is made considerably easier by concentrating rail traffic on
medium and long-distance links between major centres. Social policy
or trade union strategies should not be allowed to torpedo the necessary adjustments in railway staffing.

7) The duty of the railways to run services and carry passengers
and freight is basically a relic from the days when they had a monopoly
and is in many cases an obstacle to flexible commercial management.
Where governments think they must continue to impose this duty, the
railways should at least be allowed to decide whether they fulfil it
by means of railway or road vehicles. In the Federal Republic of
Germany the railways are at present allowed to replace certain trains
on certain sections by buses, but not all their passenger traffic.
This attitude of the authorities seems illogical. While there is much
to be said for cutting out badly utilised pairs of trains straight
away and replacing them by buses, the railways should be allowed to
transfer all their short-distance passenger traffic outside conurbations to road transport without first having to go through protracted
formalities for obtaining permission.

8) An effective brake could be put on political commitments which
handicap the railways, if the government authorities which imposed them
were in future obliged to make special compensation payments for every
increase in costs and reduction in earnings which they caused. These
authorities would then have to examine carefully whether the aims they
were pursuing were urgently necessary. The costs involved could be
better compared with the expected benefits than if all the losses were
lumped together for compensation purposes. Priorities for policy
aims can only be decided rationally when the specific costs (and the
budget funds available) are known. Railway managements should be told

what the policy aims are. Frequent changes in them would seriously
disturb the railways, handicap if not wreck medium and long-term
business strategies and create avoidable financial burdens. In
fixing compensation payments it should be arranged that all new public service obligations would at once involve specific compensation
payments by the government authorities which imposed them. This
should greatly protect the railways from additional burdens due to
such obligations. Then, specific compensation payments would be fixed
one at a time for previous obligations. The railways could influence
and speed up this process by instigating new obligations, e.g. by
applications to discontinue unprofitable services or raise politically
motivated railway tariffs.

9) Many railway companies need to adjust their organisational
structure to changed market conditions and business objectives. One
requirement is to revise responsibilities, starting with top management and continuing by setting up profit centres throughout the undertaking.

Another requirement is to make the railways act more in line with
the market as distinct from engaging in administrative activities.
Their staff structure should be geared to this aim. There is often
disproportion in the staff breakdown (into operational and administrative personnel) and a top-heavy administration. It is also necessary
to alter suitably the civil servant status of railway personnel.

Finally it should be ascertained how far railway services can be
transferred to private enterprises which could run them at lower cost
or more effectively (repair and construction work, wagon building,
etc.).

10) International co-operation between railway undertakings
should be strengthened, especially with regard to tariff policy,
operating techniques and procurement of rolling stock. On the other
hand, political considerations make it seem unrealistic at present to
consider setting up a European railway undertaking.

<u>SUMMARY OF THE DISCUSSION</u>

INTRODUCTION

As a starting point for the Round Table discussions, the main points in the Introductory Note were recapitulated as follows:

1. The diagnosis made in this Report is mainly applicable to economically advanced countries since that is where the disparity between supply and demand and the problems created by that disparity are more serious. The railways are often overdeveloped, services do not always meet the real needs of the market and demand is changing radically.

2. The fact that the difficulties are structural rather than short term makes a status quo supply policy wrong for a changing pattern of demand.

3. Some national policy objectives have also helped to bring about the present situation and to precipitate certain trends.

4. Other contributory factors sharing responsibility for the present situation are to be found in the way some railways are managed - particularly as regards personnel policy.

5. The reorganisation of freight services is inescapable. Modernisation should aim at "industrialising" goods traffic; economically speaking, this is vital but applying it will certainly raise some complex problems.

6. The pattern of freight traffic is changing rapidly both as regards location and volume and nature of the goods.

7. Greater substitutability among transport modes might nevertheless be more advantageous to rail particularly in the case of freight.

8. The production programme should concentrate on:

   - fast full-train loads between major centres,
   - switching specialised small-scale business to road services,
   - developing a simple and cheap combined transport system,

     - increasing the services offered for business and,
       to a lesser extent, holiday traffic,
     - reorganising inter-city passenger services.

9. The extent to which railways are in a position to raise fares and rates without serious risk of losing custom has become very small in some countries. It would be better therefore to aim at stabilizing earnings and cutting down on costs, a particularly difficult task in the present economic situation. It seems that the high growth years were not used as they might have been to adjust supply facilities and reduce costs.

10. Lastly, there is the question of the investment that would be required to put the above reforms into effect.

FREIGHT

The discussion showed that there were two schools of thought, one that the closure of light traffic or low volume services inevitably affects overall operating economics and the other that rationalisation it not possible through trying to attract the maximum volume of every kind of traffic. The midway view if that full trainloads will invariably be more efficient, but cannot be used in every case so that marshalling will always be necessary, although substantial reductions should be possible. Lastly, care would have to be taken not to introduce changes that are too radical because of the constraints of economic geography.

However this may be, changing over to other forms of operation (e.g. combined transport systems) would raise problems of investment, programming and international harmonization.

Demand trend analysis and specifically railway considerations point in opposite directions: trends in industrial productivity currently argue in favour of transport diversification and road transport generally fits this need more effectively.

From the railways' standpoint, a wagon's effective daily mileage is very low compared with rival modes. Even if speed is not always required by the user, much faster speeds with lower total consignment costs would seem feasible.

The basis for traffic forecasts has not been sufficiently intermodal and economic indicators have not been used enough: they have obviously been too optimistic about the railways' share in the modal split. In addition, forecasts are often designed to influence the authorities paying the grants; it would be better to inform them more accurately.

The vital need is for a big improvement in the productivity of labour. Other problems have arisen as a result of insufficient investment in the past because resources have been applied too much to operating costs and staff in particular. Lastly, government tariff policies have sometimes caused losses in revenue and not always done enough to stimulate economic choice of transport modes.

A possible objection to the recommendation for care in introducing change is the urgency of the problem, and indeed these two aspects, "care" and "urgency" will have to be reconciled if the right answer is to be found. From this standpoint, some regional economy requirements would appear to be better served by direct assistance to users; this would make action by the authorities more persuasive and selective in terms of real need than the blind support of the derived need that transport in fact is.

What is more, many users deliberately maintain private sidings as a guarantee against bad risks and also as a means of exerting pressure on rates; the costing of the private sidelines service, frequently a very expensive operation, should be more severe. The overall problem could be solved in three stages, namely:

- consider aggregate demand for all transport modes and
  break it down by these modes according to various
  transport policy options;
- introduce a policy of general reorganisation for all
  modes on the basis of these options;
- invest in all modes, again on the basis of these
  options.

Whatever policy is adopted for rail freight transport it must include measures to improve productivity and reduce costs. In particular the Round Table suggested the following methods:

- stimulation of transport between major centres through
  improvements in both technical and tariff spheres;
- cheaper and fewer trans-shipment operations by developing
  the simplest possible combined transport systems.

The Round Table drew attention to the fact that the transport business is increasingly dominated by three main ideas: a "through" service, individual treatment, and escorts. The railways must therefore fit in with this trend which reflects the fundamental requirements of demand. All too often, the railways fail, because of certain of their characteristics, to meet these requirements. In other words, their combined transport facilities do not always match up to the through-transport requirement, control of which is often in the hands of sea and road transport operators.

SMALL FREIGHT CONSIGNMENTS

The railways are uncompetitive in this area, mainly for reasons
of cost and the additional work involved. It is not even certain that
a reduction in the number of on and offloading and trans-shipment
points would be a satisfactory solution.

In some countries, this traffic has been transferred to a subsidiary with a separate accounting system and freedom as to modal
choice, the railway service offered being wagonloads between major
centres.

AUTOMATIC COUPLING

The Round Table agreed with the suggestion in the Introductory
Report and did not feel that automatic coupling was essential to future
traffic handling plans.

Too many coupling and uncoupling operations go against one of the
essential attributes of rail transport, namely bulk transport. The
manpower necessary for coupling can be considerably reduced by cutting
down train formation operations.

In the case of particularly heavy trains, conventional couplings
may not be strong enough, but there are less costly solutions than
automatic coupling such as rigid couplings or reinforced conventional
couplings.

PASSENGER TRAFFIC

The Introductory Report is less optimistic on future prospects
for this type of traffic than the conclusions of the study on the
future of inter-city passenger transport, better known as Project 33.
The main difference lies in the evaluation of future recreational
and occasional traffic by rail.

While, in the long term, travel needs will increase, the failure
of rail traffic to increase is mostly due to the fact that the services provided by other modes have improved more than rail services
have. It must be remembered that many inter-city motorway links have
been built over the last ten years and as a result the competitive
situation has changed considerably to the detriment of the railways
which have not made the same rapid progress.

It should also be noted that inter-city passenger traffic trends
in Europe vary appreciably from country to country, because of the
significant differences in commercial speeds, tariffs and the cost of
using other modes (e.g. motorway tolls).

Efforts to improve the situation should concentrate on speed and comfort. An average speed of 140 km is suggested in the Introductory Note since it is the dividing line where the competitive relationship with other modes changes but it is also the level at which costs and disamenities could become prohibitive.

For maximum speeds of over 160 km/h an entirely new track would have to be built in most cases and, at the moment this would come up against problems of cost and concerns about the quality of life. On this last point it has been pointed out that the energy and environmental drawbacks of a highspeed train would be no worse than those of the road or air transport it would replace; the psychological difficulty, however, is the fact that the environmental disamenity would arise in a new, so far unaffected, sphere.

Recreational traffic is very sensitive to fare levels and fares on some railways have now become prohibitive for certain kinds of family travel.

There are two opposing schools of thought on the economics of planning new lines. The first considers that new lines are unjustified for passengers only and that they should be routed for fast goods trains as well, which would mean less steep gradients and more bridges amd tunnels, etc.

The second theory is that the real answer in economic terms is to have a greater segregation of passenger and goods trains when available capacity becomes inadequate. Specialising in this way would improve output, simplify operation and greatly reduce the cost of the new line.

An example quoted was the cost of the new Paris-Lyon line which was F.9 million per km (including electrification) as compared with that of the new Manheim-Stuttgart line which was F.57 million per km. Though this suggests that the single-purpose passenger-only line is much cheaper, it should nevertheless be treated with considerable reserve because the land crossed, expropriations and connections to the main network are in no way comparable; the Round Table therefore gave no opinion on this example.

Since investment is generally stimulated by successful experiments, the introduction of the first high speed lines in Europe in a few years time will probably give a better idea of the possibilities they offer and the purposes for which they may be used.

LIGHT TRAFFIC ROUTES

This section also concerns stopping trains on main lines, the point being that, whilst services carrying little traffic raise an economic problem of a general kind, on busy routes output is seriously limited if slow trains with frequent stops use the same line.

The difficulty, already dealt with in other Round Tables, is not to mistake the means for the end. The regional economy can be furthered only by means of an overall development plan, not by the more or less arbitrary retention of certain rail services forming only a very small fraction of all the facilities needed for balanced development.

The right answer is to take more account of real demand, and therefore to allow it to express itself rather than imagine what it might be.

Arguments for retaining a train service are sometimes based on weather considerations or on disappointing experiences with buses in its place. One reply could be that the accessibility of a region might well be better ensured by providing it with modern slow-ploughs. As for buses, it has been found that the service has been considerably entailed after the first period of replacement. This is a matter of assessing demand correctly and, if necessary, introducing certain forms of paratransit.

The Round Table considered that regional buses should be different from city buses, particularly for relatively long trips; they should be much more comfortable and, in principle, there should be no standing.

CITY AND SUBURBAN ROUTES

While these services often meet an urgent need, there are two ways in which they could affect more commercial traffic. The financial effect might be avoided by separate accounting, but the operational effect could be undesirable if a slow train interfered with the smooth flow of other traffic; in such cases separate tracks should be provided for this type of route.

PEAK PERIOD FARES

Although it may appear economically desirable to require users that travel at peak periods and therefore reduce productivity to pay a surcharge, such a policy would seem all the more difficult to apply in that peak period trips are rarely voluntary and frequently made by the most disadvantaged social categories.

In practice, a different fare structure can be applied only in the case of a new kind of service (e.g. car sleeper trains) where it can effectively improve results by levelling out peak traffic. Superior quality services are another example (surcharge on expresses at peak hours).

The problem would be solved much more satisfactorily if the authorities did something about staggering hours. It would be helpful, for

example, to consider the positive and negative effects of various
staggering proposals in order to provide data for a better evaluation
of the possible effect of certain measures.

USERS' CHOICE

This subject gave rise to a discussion on a question of principle,
namely whether a clear and sufficiently long-term goal should not be
set for the railways. Either the reasons why we have railways are
thoroughly studied or else we dodge the issue and the railways go on
being protected without, for all that, any hope of a solution.

The answer to this question of principle is a matter of economics;
the future function depends on supply which in its turn depends on
productivity. For these elements to be properly interrelated, any
imposed liability must be specifically and fully paid for.

In the present economic situation, market economy profit margins
are whittled down and limited by policy requirements, the reasons for
which are external to the transport function. On top of this, there
are structural changes in the transport industry, and these developments are cogent reasons for selecting and defining objectives. The
latter have to be international since different national objectives
would be totally inoperable in relation to the situation they are in-
tended to cover which is mainly one of interaction and interpenetration
between the various countries.

The present problem can be seen in the conflict between the need
to cover costs and optimum railway operation of the railways. The
solution lies not so much in full coverage as in more effective coverage. Finally, it is for the community to decide how much of its
resources it wishes to spend on transport, apart from the fares directly
paid by users. For this it is often enlightening to compare a number
of objectives that could be achieved in different fields for the same
amount available for spending.

Serious distortion in users' choice arises from the differences
in social systems and working conditions in the individual transport
modes and sectors. The all-important question is whether in future
these differences will tend to lessen. Some indicators seem to point
that way; for one thing there is the increasing reluctance to work
outside "normal" working hours and days.

Some Round Table participants felt that social inequalities are
the sole concern of the company involved and are not harmful so long
as they are a matter of free choice and not a liability on the
community. In fact this creates a dilemma for if certain benefits
are met by the operator they worsen his competitive position, whereas
if they are a charge on the community they constitute preferential
treatment.

49

Another aspect which deflects the user's choice from the social
optimum is the way in which costs are computed. Railway fares are
variable and in proportion to the service rendered, whereas the cost
of using a car comprises many fixed overheads, some of which could be
made variable and thus give a more accurate picture of the real cost
of the service.

As a conjecture, for example, the fixed taxes on the purchase
and ownership of a car and compulsory minimum assurance might be replaced by an equivalent increase in the price of petrol.

Lastly, the Round Table wondered how sound was the principle of
equality when applied to modes which were sometimes fundamentally
different. Here technical aspects, historical development, political
and administrative structures, operators' objectives and many external
factors were all involved.

COVERING COSTS

A large section of public opinion in some countries is in favour
of institutionalising deficits, furthermore some thinking is in
opposition to the market economy.

The fact is that this problem needs to be seen in its real con-
text; it is an excellent means, but not an end in itself. It is a
criterion for assessing the economic utility of a product, particularly
when there are direct or indirect alternatives. To accept deficit
budgeting, therefore, means shifting the criterion to another level -
which can only be that of the overall economy. In other words, there
would have to be ways of evaluating transport services socio-
economically in comparison not only with other transport modes but
also with other products and services. For example, there is the
problem of whether to allocate resources to transport, housing or
regional planning. A last point is that the potential for increasing
productivity by organising the use of time in a society where the
tertiary sector predominates is far from exhausted; this unexplored
source has hardly begun to be tapped.

The real question for national and international communities is
to define the functions the railways should perform. The first
question to be answered is whether the market is capable of paying
for the services provided. Policy decision, for example, may be
responsible for some shortfalls in earnings. In any case, some
standard of measurement is essential. At present, there is no clear
definition of the relative responsibilities of railway administration
and policy-maker. Lastly, effective financial control implies that
there be normative budgets, i.e. budgets which pay for services
rendered and audit costs.

To meet the needs of the market in the proper way there has to
be investment. If this investment is to be planned reliably, then
commercial functions have to be differentiated from those which, for
policy reasons, are not commercial. It must be possible for investment to be broken down in the same way in order to be clearer about
which source should finance it.

The international regulations that are now being hammered out
are aimed, first and foremost, at making railway accounting more
transparent. Economic development in recent years has made the problems of transition more complicated and lengthened the time it is
taking.

Satisfactory evaluation of railway accounts should pay greater
account to certain social benefits provided by the railways, e.g. as
regards energy, smoothing out peak hour congestion, doing less harm
to the quality of life, etc.

Lastly, the Round Table felt that the identity of the decision-
maker was often confused and that this was not always conducive to
the optimum use of resources. Railway administrations make technical
and operational decisions but in many cases have no freedom of choice
as regards suppliers, wage levels, selling prices or investment
volume. Here there is a vital problem of defining respective responsibilities.

EMPLOYMENT PROBLEMS

The Round Table disagreed with the criteria used to measure the
productivity of railway personnel on two counts. First they were far
too general and lumped together unlike services where the use of
labour is not comparable, e.g. a tonne-km carried by full-train load
requires far fewer man-hours than a tonne-km carried by single wagon.

Secondly, the reference year for measuring improvement is
frequently about 1950 when productivity was particularly low.

Criteria need to be found for comparing productivity on the railways with that in other industries and services. Available indicators
suggest that the trend would not flatter the railways, in other words,
productivity would appear to have risen far more in other sectors.

Productivity should be measured in terms of standardised services, otherwise valid comparison is no longer possible over time.
From the community's viewpoint it is essential to set simple objectives on which government and railways can agree and which prevent
further social losses.

It has been found in many countries that the remuneration of
railways staff has risen at a greater rate than productivity and
faster still than revenue. What is more, there have sometimes been

big wage increases at times when economic stagnation had already set
in, helping to prolong boom conditions artificially, which partly ex-
plains the rapid deterioration of the ratio between revenue and expenditure. For instance, it has been confirmed that for the period
1970-75, unit costs for certain railways increased almost to the same
degree as energy and wages.

Recent history shows that staff reductions are contemplated and
accepted only when the financial situation is bad and the government
is under strong pressure to reduce the budgetary load.

A point here, however, is that the situation in this area differs
greatly from country to country; government aid, expressed in
monetary units per unit of output, varies considerably in different
countries.

Some rigidities stem from the guaranteed job principle, others
from inherited burdens (e.g. pensions); they cannot be changed by
the railways themselves.

It would not be realistic to try to suppress certain acquired
benefits of a statutory nature even though, in fact, they are company
benefits financed by the whole community.

It would be more feasible to plan a future policy which would
avoid further distortion by increasing disparities in remuneration as
compared with other sectors. Such a development might be encouraged
by the progressive harmonization of the regulations on all types of
transport personnel.

If existing regulations cannot be altered, there are other
methods which might gradually correct the present distortions. There
is the familiar policy of restricting recruitment to what is strictly
necessary after rationalising the production system; this possibility
is all the more realistic in that railway employees are generally in
the higher age groups and many of them will be retiring in the next
few years.

Another way of improving efficiency is to employ more staff on
really productive jobs, particularly by investing in equipment. It
is interesting in this connection to note that investment generates
jobs while improving productivity; much depends, however, on the
choice of investment.

The Round Table considered that investment should preferably be
planned so as to reduce the number of staff. Despite appearances
this is not entirely inconsistent with creating job opportunities;
the problem hinges on type of employment and job effectiveness;
furthermore, investment frequently creates short-term and eliminates
long-term jobs. Lastly, it must be remembered that investment ought
also to improve working conditions; insufficient investment under
this heading perpetuates obsolete working methods and staff suffer
accordingly.

It is essential to define an economic relationship between the
services provided and the sacrifices that the community has to make
to have them. The Round Table therefore felt that lowering costs
must take priority over employment concerns. Investment must therefore be concentrated on sectors that help to reduce costs.

Lastly, today's employment problems cannot be solved at sectoral
level. This is a societal problem and many of its aspects can be
dealt with only by general policy; there are the problems of national
solidarity, the population's increasingly high qualifications, working conditions and jobs not filled because they are felt to offer too
much discomfort. Any sectoral approach can be only temporary and
deceptive and may, in the longer term, aggravate employment difficulties since the real problems will have been neglected. Perhaps
there is a major conflict between present-day corporatism and overall
employment trends.

Apart from the fact that the safeguarding of unproductive jobs
is not a lasting solution, within a given sector it damages the sector's operational capacity, placing it at a disadvantage in relation
to its competitors and thus distorting the users' economic choice.
This also applies to all the products and services which can, to
varying extents, be substituted for transport. At two levels, therefore, resource allocation is less than the optimum and this must
affect the level of well-being.

But low productivity not only undermines the economic position
of the railways by placing them in a less favourable competitive
situation; it also mortgages their ability to adjust their technical
capacity to trends in demands. Since total budgetary resources are
comparatively rigid the one-sided demand on resources to meet the
wage bill almost automatically means that investment is reduced to
the same extent. As already pointed out, investment would enable at
least some of the staff to be employed more productively. In the
end, the effect on the company is disastrous.

Prolonged disinvestment as a result of the draining away of
resources to consumption makes equipment obsolete and so the railways
are unable to respond to the requirements of demand. Insufficient
investment - or none at all - imprisons them in a vicious circle;
the less they invest the greater the difference between what is
offered and what is wanted, which turns custom away, means lower
revenue and hence reduces the amount available for investment.
Budgetary realities being what they are and elasticity in this area
being somewhat relative, the unsuitability of the production system
leads in the long run to a further decline in financial results.
There is another aggravating factor in that since rail equipment is
relatively long-lived, the railways can technically feed off their
assets and eat them away at low cost without immediately realising

what they are doing. It is not surprising, therefore, that if this
eating away process goes on for many years the leeway that has to be
made up suddenly appears to be extremely great.

In conclusion, the workforce problem governs that of adapting
the railways to their future tasks in that the resources spent on the
former cease to be available for the latter. There is no doubt that,
in the long term, this could affect the very future of railway
workers.

INTERNATIONAL CO-OPERATION

In the view of the Round Table the railways' share of international traffic is less than it should properly be, given their
economic rates. There are many reasons for this state of affairs
and altogether they make a combination of circumstances which is not
very favourable.

First, there are capacity bottlenecks which the Round Table
suggests should be studied so as to see more clearly what would happen
if they were eliminated.

Secondly, complicated administrative procedures impede transfrontier traffic; the complication lies just as much in the railways
as it does in customs and police procedures.

Thirdly, there are too many different types of combined transport
and they are not practical enough for the user; this diversity is
frequently encouraged by national manufacturers but handicaps the
development of international traffic. Linked with this problem of
combined transport is that of commercial control, a point of sharp
contention between rail and road transport.

Fourthly, co-operation should be strengthened from the standpoint of securing business.

Fifthly, co-operation in technical planning should be improved.
The disadvantages of having national railway design offices should be
examined to see whether an international approach would not solve the
problem, since harmonisation would be possible at the drawing board
stage, thus avoiding the difficulties of harmonising after the event.

Lastly, the railways are undoubtedly at a disadvantage in the
fact that, unlike their competitors, they cannot export their services
and thus contribute to the country's balance of payments. However,
broader application of certain reciprocal or compensatory arrangements
might partly solve this problem.

Railway nationalism, whatever its origin and the reasons for it,
is now an increasingly serious handicap in providing a transport service particularly as demand is changing rapidly and in depth. International rail links, both passenger and freight, need to be both

faster and more direct, but for some passenger trains there are too
many different through carriages, which add to operating costs and
slow down the service although the demand for them is slight; the
requirement for 'through travel' therefore has to be consistent with
the need for speed and reasonable costs.

Major improvements could be the harmonisation of technical
design and better co-operation in marketing, other improvements
being more a question of the elimination of negative factors (bottlenecks, administrative complexity).

ANNEX

The Annex gives journey times over some major links with
existing trains as compared with trains on lines laid for an average
speed of 120, 140 and 180 km/h.

The table shows that in many cases an average speed of 140 km/h
would provide more attractive journey times, particularly for medium-
range evening travel and long-distance night time trips.

TIME TAKEN FOR INTERCITY RAIL JOURNEYS

Journey	Km	Present Situation (1977)		Time Taken for an Average Speed of		
		T.E.E.	Express	120 Km/h	140 Km/h	180 km/h
A. Medium Distances						
Paris–Brussels	316	2 H 20	2 H 50	2 H 38	2 H 15	1 H 45
Paris–Amsterdam	554	5 H 00	6 H 00	4 H 37	3 H 57	3 H 05
Paris–Cologne	493	4 H 50	5 H 13	4 H 07	3 H 31	2 H 44
Brussels–Cologne	226	2 H 15	2 H 25	1 H 53	1 H 33	1 H 15
Amsterdam–Cologne	260	2 H 45	3 H 25	2 H 10	1 H 52	1 H 27
Amsterdam–Brussels	232	2 H 25	2 H 47	1 H 56	1 H 35	1 H 17
Brussels–London	370	--	7 H 30	3 H 05	2 H 38	2 H 03
Paris–London	450	--	6 H 50	3 H 45	3 H 12	2 H 30
Cologne–London	596	--	10 H 40	4 H 58	4 H 15	3 H 17
Cologne–Hamburg	452	4 H 10	4 H 50	3 H 46	3 H 14	2 H 31
Hamburg–Copenhagen	360	4 H 40	5 H 05	3 H 00	2 H 34	2 H 00
Copenhagen–Stockholm	647	--	8 H 15	5 H 23	4 H 37	3 H 35
Copenhagen–Oslo	654	--	9 H 20	5 H 27	4 H 40	3 H 38
Belgrade–Zagreb	413	--	4 H 25	3 H 26	2 H 58	2 H 18
Paris–Frankfurt	646	--	6 H 12	5 H 23	4 H 36	3 H 35
Frankfurt–Milan	714	8 H 25	9 H 45	5 H 57	5 H 06	3 H 58
Cologne–Munich	635	6 H 10	7 H 45	5 H 17	4 H 32	3 H 32
Hamburg–Munich	813	7 H 30	8 H 10	6 H 46	5 H 50	4 H 31
Frankfurt–Vienna	755	7 H 35	8 H 50	6 H 17	5 H 23	4 H 12
B. Long Distances						
Paris–Vienna	1393	--	15 H 00	11 H 36	9 H 57	
Munich–Belgrade	1027	--	14 H 40	8 H 33	7 H 20	
Paris–Copenhagen	1307	--	15 H 50	10 H 54	9 H 20	
Paris–Madrid	1366	--	14 H 35	11 H 23	9 H 45	
Paris–Rome	1468	--	14 H 20	12 H 14	10 H 30	
Cologne–Stockholm	1460	--	19 H 00	12 H 10	10 H 26	

CONCLUSIONS OF THE ROUND TABLE

At the end of its discussions, the Round Table drew up the following paper which briefly sets out the main conclusions it reached. For
the most part the paper repeats the conclusions reached by the authors
in their Introductory Report; the Round Table wished to pay tribute
to them in this way for their excellent work.

As stated in the introduction to this document, the paper was
submitted to the Council of Ministers at their meeting on 6th December
1977 as one of the basic documents for their discussion on railway
problems.

Structural difficulties rather than cyclical conditions account
for the present economic situation of the railways. Solutions must
therefore be sought in a long-term view of the railways' tasks and
possibilities.

This overall view of things embraces a series of short and medium-
term measures for stabilising and adjusting the present state of
affairs:

1. Any reform measure must be based on future demand and on the
railways' technical and economic capabilities for coping with it.
Transport services should be considered in the light of the possibilities of the market and of cost structures.

2. In the case of passenger transport, rail has some good assets
for handling business trips and, to a lesser degree, for certain types
of holiday traffic. But these capabilities cannot be turned to good
account unless the standard of service is high and the average speed
sufficiently competitive; this latter requirement in practice implies
a commercial speed of at least 140 km for medium-distance inter-city
traffic. Consideration must also be given to whether fares remain
attractive for certain categories of passengers.

As a general rule, output on an industrial scale implies
homogeneous and repetitive supply in order to standardize operations
to the fullest extent: in practice this means the introduction of
regular frequency timetables and of bus services to replace rail at
lightly-trafficked stations.

3. In the case of freight, it will be essential to modify rail
transport considerably by working for more uniformity in order to
improve productivity.

Maximisation of traffic is not a sound objective since it is entirely prompted by a short-term view of things. In the long run, the problem is to carry freight economically.

To start with, it would be advisable to refrain from any further investment in installations (track, stations, marshalling yards, and junctions) when there are doubts as to whether they will continue to pay their way. On the other hand, an effort should be made to work out and introduce simple and effective combined transport arrangements which would be standardized at international level.

Rail should convert itself towards a more reliable faster and cheaper form of transport supply or a concentration of traffic in train-load lots between major nodes; however, this conversion calls for some circumspection. It has also become apparent that the idea of automatic coupling might be abandoned.

4. As regards parcel traffic, a more economic allocation of tasks between rail and road pre-supposes the establishment of specialised subsidiaries having their own budgets and making their own choices as to transport technology.

5. Where investments are concerned, due regard will have to be paid to the pattern of transport output since the simplification of the latter could bring about more efficient use of existing capacities and so dispense with the provision of additional capacity. In some cases, it could even be possible to forego replacement investments to some extent.

However, if further deterioration of the financial situation is to be avoided, rail transport supply will have to be more fully oriented towards industrial-type production, and the railways will have to equip themselves accordingly. In consequence, it may be necessary to buy heavier rolling stock and computerise rail traffic operations.

6. The productivity of labour is a crucial aspect of railway economics as it is in many cases below that of other economic sectors. In consequence, investment outlays should be largely devoted to this purpose.

Improvements could be made, for instance by better production planning and by re-organising the railway business accordingly; this implies industrial-type operations and the concentration of services.

The Round Table considered that lower costs should take precedence over employment considerations.

Employment is a societal problem which cannot be solved on a sector by sector basis without undermining the productivity of the sectors concerned and reducing the financial return available for investment which is precisely needed for readjustments to transport output. What is more, investment often creates productive jobs, and it is accordingly on these lines that the true solution of the employment problem lies.

7. Rail technology must never be prescribed as a matter of course for certain specific tasks; operators must be left free to choose the transport technologies they think fit.

8. If the community judges it necessary to impose on the railways certain assignments or obligations (e.g. not allowing them to increase their charges) with damaging effects on their profit and loss account, they should be paid compensation explicitly, as in this way the alleged benefits could be measured against the corresponding costs.

Furthermore, political objectives should fit into a sufficiently long-term frame of reference; failing this, operations are disrupted and financial costs that are not necessarily inevitable are incurred.

9. The organisation of railway networks must be brought into lines with present market conditions and with railway management objectives. This implies, in particular, the institution of financially accountable units and the introduction of cost accounting. It would also be desirable to give commercial activities more priority than administration.

Another problem in this connection is that some ancillary activities might be handled more economically by units extraneous to railway operations as such.

10. Closer international co-operation is an essential part of a new deal for the railways; it should cover tariffs, technologies and the purchasing of equipment. In particular, co-operative structures should prevent divergent approaches calling for lengthy harmonization later on. Harmonization at the planning and design stage is best.

<u>LIST OF PARTICIPANTS</u>

Mr. R. COQUAND   Chairman
Vice-Président
du Conseil Général
des Ponts & Chaussées
246, Boulevard Saint-Germain
75775 PARIS CEDEX 16 (France)

Prof. Dr. G. ABERLE   Rapporteur
Volkswirtschaftslehre 1
Justus Liebig-Universität
Licher Strasse 74, Haus 8
6300 GIESSEN (Germany)

Prof. Dr. W. HAMM   Rapporteur
Universität Marburg
Universitätstrasse 7
3550 MARBURG-LAHN (Germany)

Mr. A. AMERIO
Directeur du Service des
Affaires Générales F.S.
Ministère des Transports
Piazza della Croce Rossa
ROMA (Italy)

Mr. J.-P. BAUMGARTNER
Professor, Ecole Polytechnique Fédérale
de Lausanne
Adjoint Scientifique (CFF)
21, Chemin de Villard
1007 LAUSANNE (Switzerland)

Mr. M.E. BEESLEY
Professor of Economics
London Graduate School of Business
Studies
Sussex Place
Regent's Park
LONDON NW1 4SA (United Kingdom)

Mr. M. DJINIĆ
Secretary
Council of Transport & Communications
Yougoslav Chamber of Economy
(Privredna komora Jugoslavije)
Terazije 23
11001 BELGRAD (Yugoslavia)

Dr. J. EBNER
Bundeskammer der gewerblichen
Wirtschaft
Sektion Verkehr
1, Bauernmarkt 13
1011 VIENNA (Austria)

Mr. H. GÖZEN
Commercial Chairman of the TCDD
Bahcelievler
1 cadd. N° 27/4
ANKARA (Turkey)

Mr. J.-B. van der KAMP
Head of the Secretariat
N.V. Nederlandse Spoorwegen
Moreelsepark
UTRECHT (The Netherlands)

Mr. J. LAMBROS
The Governor
Hellenic Railways Organization
Odos Karolou 1
ATHENS 107 (Greece)

Mr. J. MIRA
Chef du Service d'Economie et
des Statistiques
Consejo Superior de Transportes
Terrestres
Ministerio de Transportes y
Comunicaciones
MADRID-3 (Spain)

Mr. R. MONNET
Directeur des Etudes Générales
et de la Recherche S.N.C.F.
88, rue Saint-Lazare
75436 PARIS CEDEX 09 (France)

Mr. H.J. NOORTMAN
Director, Stichting Economisch Bureau
voor het Weg- en Wetervervoer
Nederlands Vervoerswetenschappelijk
Instituut
Treubstraat 35
RIJSWIJK (ZH) (The Netherlands)

Mr. R.T. NORDÉN
Director
Administration and Finance
Norges Statsbaner
Storgt, 33
OSLO 1 (Norway)

Mr. J. PIETRI
Administrateur Civil
Direction des Transports Terrestres
Secrétariat d'Etat auprès du
Ministère de l'Equipement et de
l'Aménagement du Territoire (Transports)
244, Boulevard Saint-Germain
75775 PARIS CEDEX 16 (France)

Mr. R.W.S. PRYKE
Senior Lecturer in Economics
University of Liverpool
Eleanor Rathborne Building
Myrtle Street
P.O. Box 147
LIVERPOOL L69 3BX (United Kingdom)

Mr. Th. RAHN, Ing.-Dipl.
Ministerialdirigent
Haptverwaltung der Deutschen Bundesbahn
Friedrich-Ebert-Anlage 43-45
6000 FRANKFURT (M) 1 (Germany)

Prof. Dr. F. ROGIERS
Seminarie voor Economische en Sociale
Leerstelsels
Rijksuniversiteit Gent
Volderstraat, 9
9000 GAND (Belgium)

Prof. L. SJÖSTEDT
Chief Engineer
State Railways
Central Administration
(Statens Järnvägar
SJ Centralförvaltning)
105 50 STOCKHOLM (Sweden)

Mr. J.M. THOMSON
Research and Consultancy in
Transport Planning, Policy
and Economics
Kentchurch Old Rectory
HEREFORD HR2 ODA (United Kingdom)

Mr. FROHNMEYER   Observer
Principal Administrator
Division chargée des problèmes
d'Infrastructure et d'Equipement
C.C.E.
Direction Générale des Transports
Rue de la Loi, 120
1049 BRUSSELS (Belgium)

Mr. SCHMITT   Observer
Head of Division
"Prix et Conditions de Transport
et Politique de Structure"
C.C.E.
Direction Générale des Transports
Rue de la Loi, 120
1049 BRUSSELS (Belgium)

<u>Secretariat</u> : Messrs. G. BILLET
                        G. AURBACH
                        A. DE WAELE
                        F. ESTEBAN
                        A. RATHERY

ECMT

ECONOMIC RESEARCH CENTRE – FORTHCOMING PUBLICATIONS

Round Table 40:   "Paratransit"

Round Table 41:   "The role of transport in counter-cyclical policy"

Round Table 42:   "Influence of measures designed to restrict the use of certain transport modes"

Round Table 43:   Indicators for evaluating transport output

Seventh International Symposium on theory and practice in transport economics.

"The contribution of economic research to transport policy decisions"

Topic 1:   "Evaluation of demand"

Topic 2:   "Optimal use of transport networks"

Topic 3:   "Choice of investment priorities"

Part 1:   Introductory Reports

Part 2:   Summary of the discussion